Bloodhounds

A Bloodhound Dog Owner's Guide

Bloodhound Dogs General Info, Purchasing, Care, Cost, Diet, Health, Supplies, Grooming, Training and More Included!

By: Lolly Brown

Foreword

While the name might suggest a canine that's from "Horror Ville" like Transylvania, the true nature of the Bloodhound species is way different than you might expect especially if you haven't kept one before. The bloodhound breed has a reputation for being an expert when it comes to scents! Their noses can accurately detect scents and this is considered as one of their greatest distinction and strengths from other dog breeds.

Bloodhounds are not only loyal and friendly pets but they also make exceptionally useful detectives in the world of security and law enforcement. Their noses have an amazing scent detector that can accurately follow trails of the person of interest and help provide leads for investigators, and they can also provide as an aid to security personnel in various places and events. But why does the Bloodhound breed end up with such a nasty name? That's something you're going to learn later on in this book!

Bloodhounds are one of the most unique canines in a world of hounds, terriers and spaniels. They may have the nose for things but they also make great companions. They're not a breed that are usually described as "cute and cuddly" because of their wrinkled facial features but one thing is for sure, there's always more than meets the eye!

This book will guide you on how you to properly care for your pet Bloodhound dog. You'll get to learn more about the bloodhound's history, biological information, training and grooming needs, health, and the proper diet to keep your pet healthy and happy! Always keep in mind to treat your Bloodhound dog as part of your family's pack!

Table of Contents

Bloodhounds: Pet Detective

When it comes to the Bloodhound breed, we are talking about an animal with a very rich history that dates back to the Middle Ages. They were descendants of a dog breed known as the St. Hubert's Hound and also the Sleuth Hound. The breed made its mark in history through accompanying royalty on hunting excursions – thanks to their great sense of smell. Their pedigree can be traced back thousands of years, and were one of the first to earn historical descriptions and mentions ahead of other ancient dog breeds with the exception of the pugs.

Bloodhounds also have quite a strong identity prior to classification since there were some old paintings that give us an example of the breed before they were given a formal classification by dog organization like the American Kennel Club.

There were reports that the breed first made its way into the United Kingdom around the time of William the Conqueror during the Norman Conquest, though there were no official evidences or sources that can confirm it. Nevertheless, the bloodhounds were known to helped many noble man in their hunt for prey and this tradition was carried until today as they help assist law enforcements in their hunt for a culprit. There were reports before that a bloodhound breed was able to track down a criminal as far as 7 miles along a route that was heavily trafficked! I guess we can say that when it comes to keeping them as pets, you're not just getting a companion dog; you also got yourself a nosey pet detective! No wonder why many upper – scale dog keepers love to include a Bloodhound as part of their pack.

The personality of the bloodhound breed is among the best in the dog world. This canine makes a loyal house pet and a friendly companion. They have the amazing ability to sniff out prey, track down a human or animal scent and generally aid people particularly those working in law enforcements when it comes to the various aspects of the hunt. They were called as the "bloodhound" mainly because of the legendary abilities of their nose and how it accurately tracks down the blood of a wounded prey.

When it comes to getting along with his human companions, vets and bloodhound keepers highly recommend potential dog owners to take the time to properly socialize the breed so that they can get along well with other household pets including people. Since bloodhounds are large canine, they are definitely suited for older kids than younger ones because even if you get a pup, young kids may not be able to keep up with the dog's high energy.

Generally speaking, bloodhounds particularly puppies will love to play with kids of all ages but some could be quite rambunctious than others, so make sure that the personality of the pet you will choose will also suit you or that of your family members so that the dog will also be easy to get along with. If your kids learn to get along with your pet, they can surely have a great time playing with one another and this can be a great exercising opportunity both for your dog and your children.

The active energy of bloodhounds may carry on even if they are already well into their senior years though it will be much lesser than when they were younger. Bloodhounds can also get along with other household pets such as cats or dogs but you need to ensure that they are properly introduced and socialized. It's also ideal that you raise your bloodhound together with your other pets so that they will grew up together and get used to being with each other. Make sure to supervise your pet dog with another pet, be it a dog or cat, until you are sure that they're safe to be left with one another or until their relationship is already established.

We do not recommend that you get more than one Bloodhound because it may be too much to handle for most people especially if it's your first time of owning a pet dog. Bloodhounds are not for first – time owners! Keep in mind that this dog breed demands attention from their owners and requires daily exercise and mentally stimulating activities which can take up most of your time. However, if you think you can handle keeping two dogs or you already have some experience in becoming a dog owner then you can keep more than one but just make sure you can provide for both.

Should you get more than one, it's best that you acquire a male and a female – that are both neutered and spayed because if they are not neutered or spayed then they will most likely have territoriality issues or even unwanted pregnancies. Bloodhounds also tend to get into a fight if they are kept with the same – sex breed.

Chapter One: Bloodhound as Pets

The American Kennel Club describes the bloodhound breed as dignified, noble and a dog that exhibits wisdom, power and solemnity. Even though he is an easy going and gentle breed that's also sometimes quite bumbling, bloodhounds are not the lazy type of dog that you often see on TV. This large breed requires lots of space and safe areas to play around and ramble every day. It is mandatory that he is secured on a leash, or in a fence (if he is free to roam around the house) and that is because his nose just locks on to any fascinating scent that he can smell.

Once that happens, this dog's ears are turn off and it's quite impossible to get his attention back since they - or perhaps their nose, just can't resist the scent to the point that they will trail it for many miles until they get hit by a car.

Bloodhounds are generally gregarious and good – natured especially with people and other breeds but there are still some individuals that can't simply get along with other dogs and can also be aggressive to species of the same – sex.

The great strength and stubbornness of this dog breed requires a confident keeper who knows how to enforce rules in a more assertive yet not harsh manner. It's important to know that even if this breed is kind and sensitive they also have their "bad side" so you don't want to disrespect them or treat them harshly if you don't want them to become an aggressive or over – the – top stubborn as a pet.

Bloodhounds are mature in a slower rate which is why your firmness and patience should be extended over many years even if they are already an adult. This breed's tendency to chew and swallow anything that he could fit inside his mouth may at some point send you to the vet so make sure to dog – proof your house. There are also some bloodhounds that are quite possessive when it comes to toys and food which could be a potential problem if you have other pets or young children in the house.

If you want to keep a dog that is large, powerful, rugged, and with "houndy" features – long hanging ears and loose skin then this is the right one for you. Bloodhounds also have a short and easy – care coat. They thrive on vigorous activities and enjoy the great outdoors, and they have that solemn and kind yet dignified expression.

On the other hand, if you don't want to deal with a large dog that can take up a lot of space in your car or house, if you don't want to have a dog that jumps a lot and quite rowdy especially when young and if you don't want to have a pet that can be destructive when bored then the bloodhound breed may not be for you. They can get shy towards strangers especially when they are not socialized enough and they can be quite difficult to housebreak. They can also be potentially aggressive toward other animals, they are independent and have a mind of their own which is why they require an owner that is confident and can take charge. Bloodhounds also tend to drool and slobber a lot, has that distinctive "houndy" scent, loud baying and a short lifespan. Keep in mind that the inheritance of temperament in dogs is not that predictable than the inheritance of physical features such as shedding or size. The behavior and temperament will be shaped through training and the way the dog will be raised.

You can avoid some of the breed's negative traits by selecting an adult dog from a rescue group or an animal shelter. With an adult bloodhound, you can easily see the personality and temperament of the dog you are getting because they already have proven themselves that they don't have negative characteristics. On the other hand if you want a puppy, you can avoid some of these negative characteristics by getting it from a reputable source and selecting the right puppy from the litter. Unfortunately, you can never tell whether the puppy will grow up to be a well –

mannered dog or even a healthy one because it is possible to inherit health issues and temperament from the parent breeds.

Bloodhound Concerns

Here are some things that you should be concerned about if you want to acquire a bloodhound:

You need to always provide your pet with enough physical and mental stimulation.

Keep in mind that bloodhounds are rugged and large hound dogs that need enough opportunities to play and run in a spacious and enclosed area. Otherwise they can become bored and rambunctious which they usually express through loud baying and also destructive chewing. Bored bloodhounds can definitely turn your backyard and house upside – down in just a matter of minutes! We highly recommend that you as a potential bloodhound owners sign up your dogs to a local tracking club so that you can be sure that your bloodhound always get involved in potentially lifesaving activity. You see, bloodhounds were never intended to be ordinary household pets.

Keep in mind that they are working and hunting dogs which means that they have a tendency to trail scents, explore, bay and pretty much chase anything that moves, and these things can be a nuisance in a normal household setting. Trying to suppress such hardwired inclinations without providing alternative outlets for the bloodhound's energy is quite impossible and also unfair to the breed.

Bloodhounds tend to run away from its owners.

Just like all dog breeds, bloodhounds should be taught to come when you call him. However, this breed seems to have close ears and you can only count on it to obey you if he is in an enclosed space. This also means that you shouldn't trust that your pet will stay put without a leash because even if you train your dog, the risk is too great that they will literally put their nose to the ground and leave in a determined and purposeful manner seemingly oblivious to your panicky screams. The handlers of this breed used for tracking keep their pets on leash for a reason otherwise they would be out of sight in just a blink of an eye.

Bloodhounds are stubborn dogs

As mentioned earlier, bloodhounds have a mind of their own and are not pushovers to train and raise. Most bloodhounds are quite stubborn and will literally prove to you that they can do things on their own.

You need to provide them with enough socialization.

Bloodhounds need extensive exposure to sights, sounds and people because if not, they will naturally become suspicious or shy and sometimes difficult to live with.

Bloodhounds love to romp and jump

This bouncy behavior can be seen more in young bloodhounds (up until 2 years old). They love to jump and romp around (including people), and they do it with great vigor. Young bloodhounds will literally rock your world!

Potential Animal Aggression

Bloodhounds are seldom used for hunting nowadays but there are some individuals that still have instincts to seize and chase small fleeing pets but the household cat could be fine. There are also some bloodhounds that are quite aggressive or dominant towards other dogs of the same sex.

Bloodhounds are extremely noisy

Bloodhounds should never be left outside your backyard unsupervised but make sure that they are quite far from where you sleep because they are very noisy and their deep voice carries a long way.

Bloodhounds have a doggy odor and they drool a lot

Just like other hound breeds, bloodhounds possess a scent – hound which some people find disagreeable. There are some owners who are surprised as to how much their pets slobber and drool after drinking or eating, you will eventually get use to it though.

Bloodhounds have problems when it comes to housebreaking

Almost all scent – hound breeds are quite slow to pick up housebreaking concepts. You must have extreme patience during crate training because it will take them many months before they finally learn what they need to do.

Potential health issues

Just like any other dog breeds, bloodhounds are also susceptible to various health issues like heart diseases, stomach disorders, joint diseases and other health problems which we will tackle on in the next few chapters.

Good Traits of Bloodhounds

The Bloodhounds are one of the few canine breed that can be easily trained regardless of their age especially if you implement the right training methods. They usually respond to rewards and praises just like most dogs but they are known for taking pleasure whenever they do the job well. This section will cover the best traits of this hound breed. Bloodhounds are very passionate about helping authorities find the culprit, and even in doing small tasks such as trailing scents and being a good watchdog, you can definitely count on them.

Obviously you don't always need the bloodhound to sniff stuff for you, unless of course you are a police officer on the job, or perhaps you simply want to find out who ate the cake in the table! Nevertheless, you can be sure that they'll be treating you as their leader and will find whoever is behind that missing piece of cake! These dogs are at their best whenever they feel like they are involved in activities.

You won't have problems training them to behave well even if you already acquired them at a more matured age (though it may not be the case for all bloodhounds – it will still depend on the dog's individual personality).

Positive reinforcement is what works best for them as with most dog breeds. You should never punish your bloodhound in a harsh way if they don't follow your orders. Perhaps the only downside with bloodhounds when it comes to attitude is that some of them are usually shy which is why you need to train them to socialize at an early age so that they can get along well with other people and household pets as they grow. Bloodhounds respond to hand signals, whistle training, and other dog training methods.

Once you've trained them to get along with people and pets, they'll be comfortable with the family and you'll see how obedient they can become provided that you spend quality training time with them.

Bloodhounds are best suited for keepers who also love to exercise or go for a run or walk. Your dog will surely enjoy it whenever you take them on a trip around the neighborhood. The best part is that even if they have great energy they are still well - disciplined. Compared to other dog breeds, bloodhounds won't cause any problems if they're taken outside. Keepers need to provide adequate exercise opportunity for a hunting dog like the bloodhound breed. You need to take your pet out for a walk at least twice a day. If you don't have that time to take them out every day, make sure that you have a backyard where they can roam around and explore their thirst for adventure.

Bloodhounds are generally people – pleasers. You can expect them to always do their best to make you and your family happy; all they ask of course is that you give them your attention, time, and love. Bloodhound breeds sometimes go through sort of a juvenile period where they challenge their keepers for dominance and they show stubbornness which is why you need to have a firm training at this age so that you can help your pup be disciplined.

Since bloodhounds are naturally inclined to do work, and they are quite independent animals, they will usually find ways to do something such as sniffing and playing detective, so if you are not playing with them or if you don't give them something to divert their energy on. They might also end up digging your garden and backyard, or they could also end up chewing house furniture which is why providing them with exercising opportunities or playing a game of fetch at least twice or thrice a week will surely make them feel as if they are pleasing you, and it also avoid behavioral problems.

On Socializing Your Bloodhound Pup

Just like any other dog breeds, the bloodhound pups should be trained at a young age. Even if these dogs are just eight weeks old, they can already learn some good manners.

It's best to train and socialize them before they reach six months old. We also highly recommend that you enroll your bloodhound pup in a puppy kindergarten class if possible when he reaches between 3 and 4 months because this is the best age to teach them basic training and socialization skills. However, you should also be aware that many puppy training classes require the pups to be vaccinated with kennel cough or the likes; it must also be up – to – date.

There are also many vets that recommend the young pups to have limited exposure to public places and other dogs until they receive the needed vaccinations such distemper, parvovirus, and rabies and that these vaccines have been completed. In line with the formal dog training, you can already start your pups with the basics and already socialize them among friends and family while you're waiting for the vaccines to be completed. Once you already received a go – signal from your vet then you're good to enroll them to a training class. Such training and socialization experiences will help the young pup grow as an obedient, sensible, and well – mannered adult dog.

It's best to talk to an experienced and reputable bloodhound breeder so that you'll exactly know the kind of canine companion you're looking for, and how you can select the best pup. Breeders are the ones who interact daily with their pups making them the best person to ask for recommendations regarding the personality and temperament of the pups available for sale. We will give you tips on how you can select the best pup and determine a reputable breeder in the next few chapters.

Chapter Two: Acquiring a Bloodhound

There are two kinds of dog breeders; one is only concern about the money that they'll get from it while the other is more concern on how to advance the breed. The qualities you're looking for is someone who treats their litter as if it's one of their own (because it is!), and they want to make sure that their pups are going to responsible dog keepers just like them. You can easily detect which are the reputable breeders by simply asking them a couple of questions which we will tackle later on in this chapter.

If you want to get the best bloodhound breed, you have to ensure that you only buy it from a reputable dog breeder or hobbyist. This chapter will guide you on how to identify one, and also give you other options should you want to acquire from other sources. You'll also learn the purchase price of bloodhounds as well as how you can legally acquire them.

Characteristics of a Bloodhound Hobbyist

A bloodhound breeder or any dog breeder for this matter is not similar to vets because they can't be measured or judged through any form of recognition (such as license or training), or any sort of educational attainment related to breeding animals and that is because the standard of being a reputable breeder can only be seen on the temperament and general health of the pups/ dogs they raised.

Most animal breeders do this job not for the purpose of just making a quick buck but because they truly are passionate about breeding a particular canine. They have a genuine love and compassion for the dogs they breed, and always act in the best interest of the individual pups they raise.

So how can you know if you are talking to the right breeder or hobbyist? Well, you have to see if they really know what they're doing as this is the best way of finding out if they are reputable or not. Reputable breeders and bloodhound hobbyists will invest their time in knowing the knots and bolts of raising bloodhounds including the legal and medical aspects of it. In the next section, you'll find out the most important things that hobbyists and reputable bloodhound breeders should know by heart.

Key Factors to Keep in Mind

The breeder should know the importance of having a contract. This is one of the first things you should ask since it will easily weed out the legit breeders from those who are just trying to make a buck. The contract must clearly outline a refund policy and health guarantees including the bill of sale for your bloodhound canine. Speaking of which, the bill of sale is essential because this will be your proof of dog ownership. The dog ownership contract also serves as the registration and it is something that is usually filled out by the breeder. Your breeder needs to fill in the details of the breed such as sex, color, physical characteristics, date of birth, name of parents, registration numbers, and other health – related information. The breeder will need to include their name and their signature to make it valid.

Health guarantee should be your next concern when it comes to choosing a breeder. Reputable hobbyists or breeders should ensure that the breed is free from any diseases - both genetic and hereditary conditions; you may need to check if the kennel or the place where they raise the pups is sanitary, animal friendly and more than adequate for the litters because that's how you will gauge the standard of the breeder you are eyeing to buy a bloodhound from.

Another thing is breeding restrictions; dogs should be bred at least once a year only, and the current limit of per bitch is only six. It should be best that the bloodhound you're getting is either spayed or neutered. The seller might also state that the dog must not be bred until it reaches two years old, and if you plan in doing so, the breeder should be consulted first. This is usually done to make sure that other people will not breed dogs inappropriately. It's quite important because this is how the bloodline remains strong.

When it comes to lineages, the breeder should know who the parents are. You will easily know if the breeder is reputable if he/she can show you a lineage chart. A lineage chart is how you will know if the puppy came from a healthy family. Your prospective breeder must provide a lineage statement or attached a copy of the pup's lineage chart. This is very important especially if you plan on buying a Bloodhound breed for showing purposes. Speaking of showing, the breeder may indicate in the contract that the dog must be shown at least a few times per year. On the other hand, you would want to make sure that the contract guarantees that your pet can reproduce and the offspring will be free from hereditary concerns.

We also highly recommend that your chosen breeder or hobbyist is a member of a bloodhound dog club or is recognized by a breeding organization because this is an indication that they adhere to the breed's standards. It's quite common among legit breeders to improve the lines of their breed which is why don't be surprised if they will require you to notify them if ever there are any health issues that will come up after buying the dog.

They may also require for an autopsy if ever the dog suddenly dies due to unforeseen death. Most reputable breeders will also tell prospective buyers that if ever they feel like they can't handle or keep the dog for some reason the animal must be returned to them. This could mean that you cannot sell or give the pet away without first asking them; this is usually a good sign because that means the breeder you're buying from is really committed in keeping their litter safe.

Perhaps one of the best ways to really detect a good breeder is when he/ she take the time to discuss the written agreement with you and address any concerns you may have. Carefully reading the contract you've agreed to will surely make you feel confident about the Bloodhound breed you are purchasing. Legally speaking, the contract must clearly state the rights that have been agreed upon by you and your breeder. Keep in mind that the contract is a binding agreement, so before you sign, make sure that you have already asked any concerns you might have before you finalize everything. Understanding the legal aspects before purchasing a puppy or dog is part of responsible keeping and any legit breeder knows that.

Did You Know?

There are many places in the U.S. that require animals to have a health report to ensure that the puppy is getting the right health vaccinations. If you find that your pet is unhealthy, you can still return it to the breeder within 2 days. This will depend on your binding agreement with the breeder and what the law will require in your area of residence.

Purchase Price of Bloodhound Pups

Bloodhound puppies may cost anywhere between $800 and $1,200. Keep in mind that there could also be additional expenses such as shipping costs. Most legit breeders already have their litter micro - chipped prior to purchasing. The health certificates and registration papers or contract are usually included in the price of a purebred Bloodhound pup. Other factors that could affect the cost include trial performance of the pups' parents, the lineage of both parents, the reputation of the breeder itself, the color of the coat and also other forms of rarity for the breed.

Adoption Options

You may also want to consider adopting a bloodhound from a shelter. Rescue centers are built to help find new home for abandoned dog breeds. There are various rescue centers in the U.S. and also in Europe that houses abandoned Bloodhound dogs; they usually house young and adult breeds as well as senior dogs. Depending on where you live, you may find a Bloodhound that you prefer. Some rescue center will charge you with a basic fee for you to legally adopt the abandoned Bloodhound. The price will depend on the shelter or the length of time that dog stayed with them. Sometimes they will also ask an additional donation if ever the dog required a special treatment from the vet.

Most often than not, dogs from rescue centers are in poor health but because they are well – taken care of, you can be quite sure that they are already healthy and well – trained once they are adopted out. One of the advantages of acquiring your pet from rescue centers is that you already have an idea of the kind of temperament or behavior the dog has. On top of that, since vets usually volunteer to take care of the dogs in rescue centers, they are usually vaccinated and sometimes neutered or spayed already. The money you'll donate will be used to provide the needed food and medical needs for future rescue animals which mean you also get to help other pets! Win – win!

As for us and most hobbyists, the best option is to really acquire your bloodhound from a breeder that's an expert in this particular canine. It will most likely be quite expensive compared to buying from pet stores or adopting from shelters, but you can be sure of the dog's quality. There are some pet stores that sell bloodhound breeds; however, we don't recommend acquiring this canine from these places because there's usually very little information on where they came from which means that you won't be sure of its health, and most of all its personality. In addition to that, pups that are being sold to pet stores usually come from puppy mills that are mass - breeding dogs, and are not being taken care of, health wise. It's much better to adopt one or get it from a hobbyist.

There are still some personal questions you may need to ask your prospective breeder aside from the topics aforementioned but just keep in mind that the breeder you choose should be first and foremost concerned with the health and safety of their litter. They will only allow serious buyers to handle their pups. Expect them to also ask you some questions regarding your job, lifestyle or other personal topics as this is how they will know if you too are a responsible keeper and possibly worth giving their baby puppies.

Chapter Three: Is Bloodhound the Right Breed for You?

The wrinkled face of the Bloodhound might - for some reason - look adorable to you but as what people always say, looks can be deceiving; choosing the cutest pup in the litter is the most common mistake that newbie owners do which is why this chapter is about determining whether the bloodhound breed is the right choice for you. Prior to acquiring a Bloodhound, it's also best to know whether you should get a pup or a more matured dog. Taking the time to consider the pros and cons is very important at the onset in order to avoid any problems in the future particularly in terms of general care and budget.

Factors to Consider When Choosing Genders

These are the factors you need to consider when it comes to keeping a bloodhound:

- Physical Characteristics
- Temperament/ Personality
- Sexual Tendencies and Sexual Maturity
- Training and Socialization

When it comes to getting male bloodhounds, they are generally larger which means that they would eat more and that simply entails that you need to buy more food. They are also much stronger and taller than females; it could be a concern if you have other household pets that are much smaller like birds, cat or prey breeds, and because of that they also tend to be quite difficult to introduce to new pets and socialize compared to female bloodhounds. Males usually tend to be more aggressive and also independent which means that they could be quite difficult to manage especially if you live in a sort of a confined house because they won't have an outlet for their energy.

Speaking of outlet, male bloodhounds generally have territoriality issues especially if there's another male dog around. This is also true if there are female dogs around that are in their heat cycle. Males usually establish a close relationship to their owner compared to females that can equally form a bond with people other than their main keeper. Another thing is that when male bloodhounds reach sexual maturity (usually at a young age), their sexual tendencies can be a problem if you own other female dog breeds around, so don't be surprised if your male Bloodhound roams around the house or even in your neighborhood because this means that they probably have smelled a female dog that's in heat and they're pursuing it – and as mentioned in previous chapters Bloodhounds have superb olfactory senses!

On the other hand, female bloodhounds are generally less aggressive, and just like in other dog breeds, most female dogs only become aggressive when they gave birth to their pups since they are just protecting their litter. Female dogs are less active and are also generally easier to train, introduce and socialize with other household pets. They usually don't get along if they are housed with another female, and this may result to conflict which is why it's best to pair them up with a male if you want to keep two Bloodhounds.

When it comes to sexual tendencies, neutering your male bloodhound will eliminate any concerns regarding unwanted pregnancies. However, if you are interested in breeding your dog, you have to make sure that you secure him in a solid fence even if he's still small. If you buy a pair of dogs for breeding purpose, you have to make sure that you monitor the male dog because they often show aggression when a female dog is in heat. Males are naturally possessive to their female counterparts even towards its keepers. This could be a concern if you have young kids around the house, or if you don't have your dogs in an enclosure.

If ever your female dog doesn't respond to your male dog's advances, he can become aggressive. As for females their heat period occurs twice a year. It usually lasts for about three weeks. Expect to see a fluid discharge from them as this is designed to attract a potential mate. If you have your female spayed, this will prevent male dogs in smelling the heat.

When it comes to their similarities, both male and female Bloodhounds should be given equal amount of effort, time, and attention especially in socializing and training. They will require the same amount of exercise, feeding, play time, general care, housing, and love. You will need to make sure that they receive yearly vaccinations and routine checkups from the vet.

You can use the various factors aforementioned when it comes to choosing the gender of the bloodhound you want to keep. At the end of the day, choosing whether you want a male or female dog is entirely up to you. Just make sure that if you don't plan on breeding your bloodhound, it's best for them to be spayed or neutered so that they won't be pursued by other dog breeds.

Factors to Consider When Choosing the Age

Some keepers find it more advantageous to acquire an adult bloodhound because you easily know its overall appearance and size as well as its personality and behavior. Most adult dogs are socialized, trained and housebroken already which means that it can save you time and skip all the difficult parts of dog keeping, not to mention your patience and furniture. If you acquire a more matured bloodhound from a reputable breeder, the dog will most likely be trained already. You can expect him to already know how to behave around the house, on the leash, or whenever you're out for a walk.

Training is still a must but it'll be less time consuming since they're already matured compared to training a pup. Same amount of love and care is needed but less emphasis on training concepts. Most matured bloodhounds tend to be calmer when introduced to a new surrounding which is why you won't have a problem once you bring your pet home. An adult may take just a few days to adjust to its new environment so just give them time to settle and bond with them often so that they will get to establish a relationship with you and your family.

The biggest disadvantage of buying an adult dog is that it'll be harder to change any of the negative behavior they may have. If you find that your dog adapted a bad habit from its previous owner, it might be very difficult to correct. It's still possible to re – train your dog but it could be confusing for your pet. You will need to take effort if you want to change a particular habit you don't like and encourage them with treats or use positive reinforcement.

Patience is a must if this is going to be your problem but I can assure you that Bloodhounds will always try to get things right. However, if you still find that your adult bloodhound doesn't listen to you or are showing signs of misbehaving, make sure to take the time to give them positive attention and socialize with them so that they'll develop a good relationship with you.

A caveat though because there are some bloodhounds that may find it hard to settle in a new environment and this is where they usually become difficult to handle; some of them may be quite harder to introduce or socialize with other household pets, which is why you need to ensure that you monitor them whenever they're interacting with one another. If you have a smaller breed of dogs or cats, it might be more difficult as they could show dominance to smaller animals.

When it comes to basic needs, it's almost the same with puppies. Make sure that your adult dog is getting the right amount of food, has enough space where they can have exercising opportunities, and that their health is taken care of. You will need to make sure that they're neutered/ spayed to avoid any aggressive behavior or unwanted pregnancies.

On the other hand, puppies are obviously the cutest and most adorable stage in any dog's life. If you want to soak in their lovable and energetic personalities then consider getting a pup instead of an adult. Young bloodhounds will surely brighten you and your family's day the moment you wake up in the morning. Getting a puppy is best suited for individuals and families who can spend quality time with a young dog. If you plan on raising a bloodhound according to your standards, and you're focus on properly training them to meet your requirements, then you'll have better chances with a pup compared to an adult.

You need to spend quality time with your pup and form a bond with them so that they will be easier to train or socialize. Some people get a pup but they are not in the house all the time or they don't take the time to train them, and they wonder why their pets are misbehaving. If you want your bloodhound to become a well – behaved pet as it grows, you must give time and attention to it, and not just provide their basic needs. Purchasing a puppy from a reputable source or rescue shelter will make the dog stay longer as part of your family since it'll recognize that you're the one providing them with all their basic needs and general care as they grow. They'll recognize that they are part of the pack.

Prior to buying a puppy from the breeder, it is best that you take the time to see how they interact and play with other dogs as this will give you a hint when it comes to temperament. Usually, puppies that grew in a litter tend to be more assertive and aggressive than puppies that are raised alone which is why the former might be harder to train. The latter though may tend to be more reserved especially with strangers, which is why socialization at an early age is important.

Some owners find it difficult to manage and raise a pup especially if they have their own families to take care of. You have to keep in mind that raising a puppy whether it's a bloodhound breed or not is very similar to having a baby. You are responsible every single day especially in the first few months. You need to also ensure that you have the time to let your pup meet new people, other pets, and take them out for a walk around the neighborhood.

As puppies grow, you'll soon find out that they also become quite stubborn just like a child. If you're sort of a neat freak and you want everything organize around the house, getting a puppy may not be best for you because at some point they can damage your furniture and other household items especially when they undergo the chewing stage. You need to puppy – proof your house and also housebreak your pup. When it comes to training, if you want it to be effective, you have to be consistent with your methods and the schedule otherwise it could be difficult for you these wrinkled cuties!

Purebred or Mix Dog Breed?

The decision of getting a purebred bloodhound dog over a mixed breed or a crossbreed should be after you hear both the positives and negatives. There are lots of books and online resources out there that only discuss the positives but leave out the negatives. You might be convinced that you want a purebred dog but often times, people who choose purebred dogs are only basing their decisions on the pros without considering the cons. This chapter will provide you with a more balanced perspective about purebred dogs so that you'll know the truth about their characteristics and traits as well as the advantage and disadvantages of keeping one so that you can make a wise and informed decision.

Advantages of Acquiring a Purebred Bloodhound

One of the major advantages of a purebred dog is that you can easily predict its physical as well as behavioral traits. Puppies grow up and look a lot like their parents despite each of them having their own unique set of genes. Just like in humans, the genes produce the desired traits for a particular breed – in this case a Bloodhound dog. The desired traits usually include the color, coat, erect ears or not, size of the breed etc. The breeders are the one who ultimately decides which traits are desirable, and they will try to produce those traits as they further develop a particular breed.

When breeds with the wanted characteristics are developed, the genes that have such traits will spread throughout the gene pool of that particular breed. For instance, when you see a puppy that's a member of a certain breed, you'll have an idea which genes or desired traits were inherited. If you prefer to acquire a certain length of coat, or dog size, you can choose a breed that carries the genes of such traits. For many people, the appearance is the most predictable trait of purebred dogs.

Genes also carry some aspects of behavior and personality. For instance, bloodhound is known for accurately trailing scents; this means that the breed inherited genes with such extreme olfactory senses. You can choose dog breeds that carry genes with your desired personality/ behavioral traits such as dog breeds that are known for herding sheep, watchdog, rodent hunters, or in the Bloodhound breed's case someone that is hardworking and loves to hunt for prey.

You can choose a dog breed that tends to inherit such kinds of temperament. However, keep in mind that some behavioral and personality aspects are not inherited, instead it is more based on the dog's environment – how they are raised and trained since they were young. There are some dogs that are more affected by their genes while there are some that are more affected by how they were raised.

Another thing you need to keep in mind when it comes to behavioral traits is that these are already hardwired in your dog's genes which mean that it can be hard to change. Therefore, in order to minimize stress and struggles on your part, you should look for a breed or a puppy that already possess a temperament you prefer or something that you can handle.

There are many newbie dog keepers that acquire a purebred dog and then complain later on about its natural traits. This is why it's very important that whenever you choose a certain breed as pet; you need to make sure that you can handle its physical traits and characteristics. As with bloodhound dogs, you'll most likely have a problem with their chewing and the need to do something since they are used to exploration and vigorous activities. Other breeds are somewhat the same; they are developed to do some type of work like hunting rodents or rabbits, herding cattle, guarding the livestock, pulling sleds or carts, aiding law enforcements and the likes. So if you just want to have a family companion or a lap dog, purebred canine is definitely not for you. Their working traits can be a nuisance for you so make sure to consider that aspect.

Some behavioral traits that helped a purebred canine do its work include their high energy level so make sure to keep up with them as they can get bored easily if you don't prepare any activities or spend time with them; independence which means it can be hard for them to follow what you want because they are clever and have a mind of their own. They also have a strong desire to do hunt or work and they can also exhibit nipping, aggression (especially towards same sex breed) as well as barking.

Many purebred dogs don't guarantee that they act or look the way you expect. A purebred pup can grow up to act or look differently than what you expected. The predictability factors that we've discussed earlier are typical but not always guaranteed. Just like humans, there are some purebred canines that do not "conform to the status quo" of their breed. When it comes to genetic health issues, there are various genetic health issues that occur in dogs but it's not just limited to purebred canines. Such issues can affect mix and crossbreeds though the risk of these health problems usually occur more in purebred canines than in mixed breeds or crossbreeds.

All in all, a purebred dog may be right for you if you know the characteristics and traits you want in a breed; if there is a dog breed that has all or at least most of the traits you're looking for and that it's something you can handle; if you will gladly accept the other undesirable traits that the breed may have; if you're willing to accept the risk of health issues; if you are willing to pay a certain amount to acquire a puppy from a reputable source, or have the time to adopt a dog from a rescue shelter; if you are willing to acquire a puppy from someone who you know produces healthy and good – tempered purebred canine.

Your pet's temperament needs, and behaviors will definitely change as they age. As much as you want your bloodhound to stay as active as they are when they're still young, this aging and slowing down is obviously inevitable. There are some things that you can as their owner to make the inevitable manageable. The most important thing to keep in mind is to keep your pet active. Make them feel young at heart by involving him everything you or your family do and never stop being creative when it comes to creating routines for your bloodhound.

Chapter Four: Bloodhounds Must - Haves

Bringing home your new bloodhound pet will surely be an exciting time for you and your family. When it comes to bringing home a full – grown or matured dog doesn't need quite as much attention compared to bringing home a pup. Adult bloodhounds are usually house - broken already and some are also trained and well – behave. However, you still need to take precautions and let your pet adjust to its new environment. On the other hand, bringing home a puppy is going to be a different experience compared to bringing an adult one home.

If you want to avoid getting frustrated and exhausted once your new pup arrives, it's better to plan ahead of time and prepare your house for him. You will need to puppy – proof your home in order to provide a hazard - free environment for your young pup. It will take only just a few hours to make your house safe once your pet arrives. Puppy – proofing will set the tone for you and your pup's relationship, and will create a proper introduction to the family as well.

This chapter will cover some tips on how you can help your new pup or matured dog make the transition to its new home. You'll learn the basic supplies they will need and guidelines on how to puppy or dog – proof your house to keep them safe from any potential harm inside the household. Learn about what to expect once they've finally set their paws into your home.

Precautions When Bringing Home a Bloodhound Pup

First time dog owners aren't usually aware of how challenging the first few days can be especially when bringing home a young pup. Before bringing your puppy home, it's important that basic supplies are already prepared because this will make your puppy feel safe. Make sure to ask the breeder or previous owner as to what kind of diet the puppy was raised in, especially if the pup has any other special requirements.

You see, having a puppy is just like having a newborn baby in the house which is why you need to make sure that your house is safe because they are naturally curious at this stage and will definitely go through everything. Simple cords or hanging curtains can be a hazard for your nosey pet. Some of the things you need to do before your puppy arrive include picking up cords or any kind of strings lying around the house. These materials can easily be swallowed by your pet and can definitely cause gut problems. You should also remove any choking hazard such as small pieces of toys or something similar must be removed because your pup will be curious enough to swallow them. Electrical cords or any potentially hazardous material should be out of reach and must be secured; this includes matches, lighters, and fire extinguishers. What you can do is to spray a no – chew product to the cords or other materials though it will be a bit unpleasant for the puppy. Never let your puppy access them if you want to make sure that you still have a house to come back home to. Remove any poisonous houseplants; if you have cactus inside the house, make sure it's out of reach. You should also keep the puppy lock up inside its kennel if you're going to be out for a while or if you're unable to watch the puppy. Make sure to provide food, water and toys.

Puppy Supplies

In addition to puppy – proofing your house, you need to also prepare the basic supplies that your puppy will need at least a few days before its scheduled arrival. You'll also need to prepare yourself because working with puppies can be quite exhausting as well. Having the right attitude and a plan especially when it comes to feeding, exercising, grooming, training schedules and other necessities will help you get things in order and save you time. The key is to enjoy the caring process, and just give these wrinkled bloodhound pups some love! First off is to ask your breeder if the puppy already began training, if so, then make sure to continue the training to avoid confusion with the already established commands. You should also buy a dog crate that is at least twice as large as the current size of your pup. When it comes to bedding, we recommend that you purchase quality bedding that can't be easily destroyed. Make sure it's washable because it'll be prone to your puppy's litter.

You need to also buy a woven puppy collar; you can also choose materials that are made out of soft fabric. Make sure that the collar you buy has a buckle fastener so that you can fit your puppy's neck without it being too loose or tight. A good measurement is if you can easily insert your 2 fingers between the collar and your pup's neck. Quality lead is also a must especially when you take your pup out for a walk. It's highly recommended that you buy a retractable type of lead to make the dog easier to handle. To complete it all, you will need to get your pet a tag because it will serve as identification if ever your puppy gets lost. Make sure to put it on their collar and include your contact details so that your puppy can be easily returned to you. This is a must even if your dog is already micro – chipped.

When it comes to grooming since bloodhounds are shorthaired, you won't need lots of grooming tools. Make sure to ask the breeder regarding what age you can start to trimming your puppy's coat. Usually, you need to wait until the puppy is already 10 months old. Ask your vet or breeder about it.

You will also need to buy toys. This is a must both for pups and even dogs because it will keep dog boredom at bay and it'll keep them occupied if you aren't available to play with them. The toys should preferably be plastic and doesn't become a choking hazard. If your puppy is happy with the toys you provide him, he will refrain from chewing household items or furniture. You need to also make sure to have good quality of food once your puppy arrives. You need to ask your breeder as to what kind of diet your pup has and try to continue that by buying the same brand or offering the same amount. If you want to change their diet, make sure to do it in a gradual way so as not to upset your puppy's stomach. What you can do is to combine the old diet with the new so that transition is gradual. Let your pup adjust to the new diet to prevent diarrhea.

Since pups are quite active animals, you need to make sure that you buy a food/ water bowl that can't be easily tipped over. Make sure to replenish clean water two times a day. Some keepers use automatic feeders but it's just optional. If you want to confine your pup in one area then purchasing baby gates is very ideal. This will prevent your curious pup in accessing restricted areas around the house. Lastly as mentioned earlier, you may need to buy a spray – on "no – chew" products. This will come in handy if your pet is fond of chewing one of your furniture or any potentially hazardous material.

Precautions When Bringing Home a Bloodhound Dog

If you are keeping other household pets, it's best to separate your bloodhound once it arrives to avoid any fights. Once you've properly socialize your dog with your family, you can start introducing him to your other pets but do so with precaution and make sure that you monitor their interaction. It's also best for you to dog – proof your house at least until you already have an idea on how your bloodhound behaves around the house. Remove any chewable items or any appliances that they can get caught up in. Secure electrical cords and anything that's hanging as well as the food in your kitchen. Once your dog already demonstrated a well – behave manner, you may place the items back in the room.

If you have children around the house make sure to supervise them when interacting with your bloodhound. The dog may be quite wary at first and will need to adjust before your kids can freely pet or play with them. Adult bloodhounds are not advisable for very young kids since they are large and are natural hunters. Make sure to not stimulate or over excite your dog at least for the first few days so that they can properly adjust.

Supplies for Your Adult Dog

Just like puppies, your adult dog also need supplies like food and water dishes, kennel, (washable) bedding materials, collar, lead and dog tag, toys and of course quality dog food. Most keepers prefer that their dog stays in his or her kennel and not just let the dog sleep anywhere in the house but this of course is up to you. However, providing a kennel will make your bloodhound feel safe and comfortable. For bloodhound dogs, you can use a chain collar but make sure to be careful with it as it could hurt your pet if you pull them off while walking. This is why retractable leashes are preferred because your dog will have freedom to roam around while you're still maintaining control over its movements.

What to do after Bringing Your Bloodhound Home

After a few days of adjustment, you can start housebreaking or housetraining your dog. One of the first things you need to do is to praise him. Keep in mind that your voice is first and foremost your training tool. You need to also consider using a consistent phrase to cue your pet to go inside its crate. Pairing a word or phrase will help when you're instructing your pet and catching their attention towards where it needs to be.

You should initially use a lock or something so that the door wouldn't swing back and forth so that it wouldn't scare your bloodhound. You can also lure them with toys and treats. Make sure to keep a bowl of treats when you're doing crate training as it will be handy and can also function as pre – bait for your dog. Chew toys is also essential because you'll need to reward it afterwards. Never crate train your dog if you don't have food and toy rewards. You must set it up beforehand so that it can be convenient for you once you start training your bloodhound.

Make sure to avoid following a strict routine when crate training your pet. Routines are great but make sure that your training follow – up is not predictable for your pet. What you need to do is to destabilize any pattern that will short – circuit your dog's expectation. This way it will help preserve the integrity of your crate training.

As you now have learned, housetraining is quite a labor intensive task but it lessens the onset of many problems in the long run. Observe your dog as it will have its own pace of learning. You need to be patient and continue practicing your pet to go to the crate willingly. It may probably take several days to a few weeks or maybe even longer so don't rush it.

Protection for Your Bloodhound

If ever your dog got into an accident or acquired an illness, you can take him to the vet or a specialist but it is much better if you get him protection policy called a pet insurance which is similar to getting your own health insurance.

Your bloodhound pet basically gets treatment if he acquires any illness or experienced some sort of accident. Needless to say, the insurance company pays most of the vet bills. Unfortunately, family health insurance doesn't cover household pets even if we can all argue that they are all part of your family's pack. This is why pets have their own policy that can protect them should the need arise. Usually, pet insurance companies pay more than half of the bills and the rest is paid by the owner; this known as co – pay. There is also a deductible wherein the owner shoulders the payments temporarily before the insurance payment and co–pay are calculated. If you have chosen a higher deductible or co–pay that means your monthly premium is less. Some owners choose to have a lower co–pay or deductible and they let the company pay more for the final bill. This is up to you to choose the best policy for you and your bloodhound water dog.

Chapter Five: Controlling Bad Habits

In addition to socializing your new Bloodhound breed you should also begin training as soon as possible. Bloodhounds are very intelligent and patient dogs, which is why starting with training early will increase your chances of having a well-behaved and obedient adult dog. When it comes to dog training, there are many different methods to choose from that we will tackle later on in this chapter. You will also learn how to properly manage and handle your dog's potential behavioral problems. Keep in mind that training them at an early age is one of the most important things you need to do to avoid or prevent such misbehaviors.

Basic Training for Your Bloodhound Pup

When it comes to training your pup, consistency is essential. Tolerating their bad habits will only make the situation worse, and it'll be harder for you to correct them so make sure that you talk what you preach. Try seeking out a professional trainer to help you out if you have difficulties in managing your bloodhound's behavior.

One of the first things you need to teach your pet is reward reinforcement. This method of training hinges on your dog's natural desire to please. In essence, you train your dog to repeat desired behaviors by rewarding him for doing them. For example, if you want your dog to sit, you just don't command it; you must teach him what the command means and then reward him each time he responds to the command appropriately.

Reward reinforcement training is one of the most popular and effective dog training methods. Another thing you can do is by using a clicker. This type of training is a version of reward reinforcement training and it is also highly popular. The key to success with reward reinforcement training lies in helping your dog identify the desired behavior and that is where the clicker comes in.

You go through the normal process of training, giving your dog a command and guiding him to perform the desired behavior. Then, as soon as he displays the behavior you click the clicker and immediately issue a reward; this helps your pet to learn more quickly which behavior it is that you desire. However, you should only use the clicker during the first few repetitions of a training sequence until your dog learns what the desired behavior is because you don't want him to become dependent on the clicker to perform that behavior.

When it comes to punishment, it can also be a type of training but obviously is the opposite of reward reinforcement training. Rather than rewarding your dog for performing desired behaviors, you punish him for performing unwanted behaviors. The punishment used doesn't have to be violent or cruel – and it shouldn't be! But from time to time, you can do simple punishments such as withdrawing your attention to teach your dog to stop whining. Give your dog the opposite of what he wants to curb out the negative behavior in question. This type of training is more effective as a method for curbing negative behaviors than for teaching positive behaviors.

Good Barking vs. Bad Barking

Some types of barking are encouraged by most keepers especially if there's a stranger in the house or perhaps a threat. On the other hand, bad barking are less desirable and should be controlled but before you do that, your dog must first understand the difference between good barking vs. bad barking, and you'll need to incorporate that during training.

You should also teach you bloodhounds about controlled barking. Obviously this is something that dogs are naturally inclined to do but there are some that just go over too much. It often occurs as a response to a certain situation rather than for the mere sake of them trying to be loud. Whenever a dog barks it's either they're very excited or scared; if the barking is driven by fear, it's their way to try to get your attention or as part of their defense mechanism. Most of the time if a dog is barking, they're just trying to intimidate whatever or whoever is making them fearful. Some instances include if there's a stranger or a completely unfamiliar face in your house, garage, or territory; ringing doorbell, unfamiliar sounds, if there's another pet or animal lurking around and if they are bored or want to play with you.

Nuisance Barking

You can create interventions in order to control your bloodhound's barking though most experts say that it's definitely much easier to train your pet when is the right time to bark compared to training them when not to bark. There are some dog breeds that are natural barkers which means they bark just for barking's sake - this is also known as nuisance barking. Fortunately, it doesn't include bloodhounds. As always, we do not recommend punishing your dog for its excessive barking because it's highly ineffective and will only make the problem worse. What you can do to control the barking is to distract him/ her and then reward your bloodhound for following your orders of silence. Make it repetitive every time they bark for no reason. Increase the reward as they learn how to hold silence longer; this way you're training your pet that short barks are okay with you.

As mentioned in previous chapters, make sure to start training and socializing your Bloodhound at a young age. Socialized pups tend to bark less because they're already used to having new people around and they can easily adapt to different situations. Make sure to keep your pet busy by providing variety of toys because sometimes barking is caused by plain boredom. If you can't seem to handle the problem or you have no time in doing repetitive activities, you can always hire a professional trainer or enroll your pet in a training class in order to resolve this issue.

What you can do to train and control your dog's barking behavior is to have a known person knock at your door. Then let your bloodhound bark at least once or twice before giving the quiet command. Next step is to open the door and let the person come in. You can then give a reward if your bloodhound doesn't bark at the familiar face. Make sure to repeat this activity a couple of times so that your pet will learn that not everyone who knocks at the door is a total stranger or a threat. Reward your pet every time it stops barking as it acts as a distraction from their barking itch. You can also use an empty soda can and fill it with pebbles and shake it every time he stops barking as a form of distraction before you proceed on giving treats. If you can't seem to handle the problem or you have no time in doing repetitive activities, you can always hire a professional trainer or enroll your pet in a training class in order to resolve this issue.

Do Bloodhounds Bite?

If they considered a person or another animal a threat then yes they do and they won't even hesitate about it. As long as you're not a threat, they won't really bite you though some dogs have a habit of biting and nipping which is something that can become a very disturbing habit that your Bloodhound can develop if not prevented early on. This kind of behavior is not just distracting for you or other people; it can also lead to your pet being confiscated if ever it bites a child or a stranger. In order for you to better understand your pet; you have to know the probable reasons why he/she is doing it in the first place.

One of which is because they want to show dominance to other pets or to simply gain your attention. Another common reason is when puppies are usually removed from their mother and siblings too early tend to become a biter or nipper because they were not properly socialized with their own kin. In a litter, puppies play with their siblings through nipping one another so they've learned early on that biting another puppy is a form of affection. However, if the pup is removed early, he/she will not understand the process and will just bite because he wants to.

Most owners make the behavior worse because they allow their pups to buy or nip them while playing. You should only allow your pup to bite their toys during playtime and not you. Biting and nipping may also be a sign that your pet is suffering from an illness or he/she is in pain.

It's very important to also determine and consider why your pet is doing this at the moment because it might be an isolated occurrence and not misbehavior.

Some methods that can help train your Bloodhound pup to lessen the nipping or biting is to play with your pup as you normally would, and if your dog starts to nip/ bite , stop him/ her and say "no" in a firm but not in a scolding way. Don't interact with your pet until it is calm. Another way is to yell "ouch" whenever your pup tries to bite/ nip you, and then ignore him/ her. Most pups will respond to this kind of treatment.

When you start playing with your pup again, make sure to provide a toy whenever he/ she tries to nip on you so that it can be re – channeled to the toy. You can also try offering your hand, and if ever your pup doesn't bite you anymore, praise him for the good behavior and reward him with treats. However, if your pup tries to get your hand and nip you, what you can do is form a fist so that your pet will let go of your hand as this is uncomfortable to their mouth. Offer a toy play instead.

If you want to stop your pup nipping at your heels, try carrying a spray bottle of water and loudly say no, then spray him/ her with the water. Place him inside the crate for around 30 minutes if ever he/ she is still following you around and nipping at you. However, don't use the crate as punishment; just place your pet there to calm him down. Close the door but don't lock it.

Once your pup is all calmed down, you can walk him/ her outside before trying to pet it again. You can also offer up a toy before your pup even think about getting into the biting or nipping you. Make sure to avoid any games that involve biting such as tug of war, chasing games etc. at least until the pup is already matured enough to distinguish your hand and their toy.

When it comes to controlling an adolescent Bloodhound to stop biting or nipping is much harder to do, and it may also be associated with health issues. Make sure to bring your dog to the vet to check if your dog has some kind of illness or nervous disorders. Usually, if there are new pets around the house, your dog may tend to get stressed out thus the biting. What you can do is to isolate your dog for the mean time, and give it time to adjust to a new pet or perhaps to a new situation at home.

You should correct the biting before it becomes a pattern. Speak firmly and use the spray water method to correct the issue. Keep your dog away if you see that it always try to bite or nip at other people until after you've dealt with this kind of behavior. If this is a recurring behavior and you find that it's not due to any health issues, the best option to take is to enroll your dog to a training class or hire a professional to do the job for you. You can ask your vet or your breeder for recommendations as well. The key in handling undesirable behavior is learning how to work with your dog and being consistent with your training

Controlling Aggressiveness

One way of showing aggressiveness is through jumping. It is also a problem in most canine breeds especially during the adolescent stage or juvenile pups. This is a period where your pet gets so excited whenever they see people around or if other pets are nearby. They will attempt to jump on you or other animals in an effort to get your attention. Usually, jumping is a nuisance behavior and can be quite dangerous for seniors and very young kids. It can also be quite irritating if your bloodhound always jumping on you or constantly knocking things off your hands.

As always, the best way is to start them while they're still young. Never reward or recognize your pup whenever they jump on you. Avoid the temptation of always trying to make them jump on you so that they will not get used to it. If you want to pet them, reach down to them or just hold them towards you, and don't do any motion or command that will provoke jumping towards you. Once your pup stops jumping, make sure to praise them or give them treats. However, if your find that jumping is part of your bloodhound's personality, what you can do is to eliminate rough plays with them such as wrestling.

You can channel your pet's playfulness towards a toy rather than you or other pets and people. Always reward your pup with a treat and a positive praise. If you have other housemates, make sure to talk to them about the behaviors that are acceptable, and those that are not so that they will not send mixed messages to your pet about the right and wrong behaviors.

Adolescent dogs are a bit harder to train than a puppy. Most of them also jump in an effort to get your attention, and if ever it wasn't corrected at a young age, jumping will become a nuisance to them. What you can do if your bloodhound is six months and older is to use a leash training method. You will need to ask another person to help you out as this requires two people. One person must hold the dog while on a leash, and the other approaches the bloodhound. If your dog tries to jump up and greet you, what the handler should do is to tighten the leash and command the dog to sit. Do not give the dog the opportunity to jump. If your pet succeeds, both of you should praise him and give rewards. Doing this can result to a well – behaved dog and they will learn how to properly greet a person.

If you do the method above to a much younger bloodhound, the handler may have to sit on the floor so that he/ she can control the jump from happening. The key here is to be consistent. Your bloodhound will not understand what you're trying to teach them if you or other people allow a bad behavior like jumping and then reward or punish the dog for it. Ask other people or your family to interact with the dog in the same way that you train them.

Chapter Six: Bloodhound Breed Standard

The Bloodhound is a breed that possesses every characteristic and point of those canines that hunt together through scent. In a most marked degree, this breed is very powerful and can stand over more ground compared to other hound breeds. Their skin is extremely loose and thin to the touch which is more noticeable around the neck and head area where it hangs in deep folds. In this chapter you'll get to learn the official breed standard of Bloodhounds as well as the advantages of purchasing a purebred dog and also some grooming tips to keep your dog in good shape.

Bloodhound Dog Official Breed Standard

Height

The average height of adult Bloodhounds is 26 inches while adult bitches stand at about 24 inches. Male breeds usually vary from 25 to 27 inches while bitches vary from 23 to 25 inches; in both cases, greater height is preferred in combination with its quality and character.

Weight

The average weight of an adult male Bloodhound is 90 pounds while an adult – size bitch is at 80 pounds. Some males can attain the weight of around 110 pounds, and some bitches can reach up to 100 pounds. Just like the height, greater weight is preferred but this time it is in combination with its quality and proportion.

Expression

- The expression of the bloodhound breed should be dignified and noble

- It should also be characterized with wisdom, power and solemnity

Temperament

- When it comes to the temperament, bloodhounds are very affectionate to its owners.
- The breed is also not quarrelsome with other pets and dog breeds
- The nature of bloodhound is shy and sensitive. He is also sensitive to correction or kindness of his keeper.

Head

- The head of the bloodhound breed should be narrow in proportion to its length and long in proportion to the body.
- The head should also be slightly tapering from the temples to the end of its muzzle so that when the dog is viewed from above and in front it will have an appearance of being flattened at the sides while being nearly equal in width throughout its entire length.

- In profile, the upper outline of the breed's skull should be nearly in the same plane as that of its foreface.

- The length from the end of nose to the midway portion between its eyes (stop) shouldn't be less than that from its stop to the peak (back of its occipital protuberance).

- The entire length of its head from the posterior part of the occipital protuberance to the end of its muzzle should be around 12 inches (or more), and around 11 inches (or more) in bitches.

- The skull should be narrow and long, and its occipital peak should be very pronounced. The brows should not be prominent although owing to the deep – set eyes, they could have exhibit kind that appearance.

- The foreface should be long, deep and should have an even width throughout its square outline when seen in profile.

Eyes

- The eyes should deeply sunk in its orbits

- The lids should have a lozenge or diamond shape in consequence of its lower lids being dragged down and averted through the heavy flews.
- The eyes generally correspond with the general tone of the breed's color that could vary from yellow to deep hazel.
- The hazel color is preferred although it's quite seldom to be seen in liver – and – tan bloodhounds.

Ears

- The ears are thin and soft to the touch
- It should be extremely long and must be set very low
- It should fall in the side of the head in graceful folds (with the lower parts curling inward and backward).

Mouth

- Scissors bite is preferred
- Level bite is accepted

Wrinkle

- The head is furnished with an amount of loose skin

- Every position should appear superabundant especially when the head is carried low.

- The skin should into loose, folds, and pendulous ridges particularly over the sides of its face and forehead.

Nostrils, Lips, Flews, and Dewlap

- The nostrils should be open and large

- The front of the lips should fall squarely so that it can make a right angle with the upper line of its foreface

- Hanging and deep flews should form and it should be continued to the pendant folds of loose skin around its neck that can constitute a pronounced dewlap.

- In bitches, these characteristics should be found in a much lesser degree.

Neck, Shoulders and Chest

- The neck should be long and the shoulders should be muscular and well – slope at the back

- The ribs should be well – sprung

- The chest should be well let – down that could form a deep keel between its forelegs.

Legs and Feet

- The forelegs should be large in bone and it should be straight
- The elbows should be squarely set
- The feet must be well – knuckled up and strong
- The thighs as well as the gaskins (second thighs) should be very muscular
- The hocks should be well bent, squarely set and properly let down

Back and Loin

- The loins should be deep, strong and slightly arched
- The back should be strong while the stern should be long and tapering
- The stern should also be set on a high but with fair amount of hair underneath it

Gait

- The gait should be swinging, elastic and free

- The stern should be carried high though not too much curled over its back

Color

- The color of the breed can be red, black and tan, and liver and tan.

- Darker shades should be interspersed with a badger – colored hair or something light that is flecked with white

- A small amount of white is allowed on the feet, chest and tip of its stern

Grooming Your Bloodhound

Ideally, your Bloodhound should take a bath at least thrice a month or when it's really necessary since they have that "houndy" scent. Canines don't like bathing in general especially if you're living an area where there are really cold temperatures. Some keepers bathe their dogs every other week or more, but it is entirely up to you and the living condition you have.

Short – Haired Bloodhounds

Since Bloodhounds possess a short – haired coat, you don't need to do regular brushing compared to other dog breeds. However, you still need from time to time brush any loose fur especially before bathing them. You can brush their coat a bit before soaking it with water. Blow drying can also blow away the residue and loose fur in your pet's coat.

Keep the coat smooth and clean by using dog toiletries such as towel, rubber mat, shampoo, soap, water and other dog – friendly grooming materials. You need to also make sure that you provide a rubber mat or a towel to prevent him from slipping off. If you're going to bathe your bloodhound outside, it's really not necessary to put a rubber mat but it can still be useful. Once you did that, make sure to wet your dog with lukewarm water. It'll probably take around ten minutes to wet him all over.

You can now apply the dog soap or dog shampoo. However, before you do make sure that it's diluted with water. After you rub and bathe your dog, it's time to rinse him off. Make sure that there's no trace of shampoo left as it could irritate your pet and make him itch. Dry him off and use a blow dryer to dry the water on his skin.

Keep in mind that the shampoo or soap you use must be dog – friendly, and doesn't have strong ingredients. Never use your own shampoo as this could be harmful for your pet. You should also be careful when applying the shampoo near their eyes.

Cleaning Your Bloodhound's Ears

You definitely need to clean out your bloodhound's ears since they are lop which means that they are susceptible to bacteria – build up. You may ask the vet first to show you the correct way in doing it to avoid harming your pet. Whenever you're cleaning your pet's ear, make sure to check the hair around the ears and inside the ears to see if there are any signs of ticks and mite infestations. If ever there is, you can immediately remove them and dab with antiseptic solution.

Preventing Tartar Build - Up

Keeping your dog's teeth and gums clean and free of any tartar is essential to its health because it can help improve their digestion and also prevent any internal illnesses. A healthy gums and teeth will enable your bloodhound to properly eat their food which can help in proper digestion. You can ask your vet or your breeder to show you how you can properly and carefully brush your pet's teeth. Usually when you take your dog out for a check – up, your vet will clean your dog's teeth and scrape off the tartar.

Declawing Paws

When it comes to declawing, you need to trim your pet's nails at least twice or thrice a week using nail clippers that's suitable for your bloodhound. You want to make sure that you always check your dog's nails, and get him accustomed to your handling in order to make them feel at ease whenever you're clipping its nails. You need to push back the skin and make sure you can see the part of the nail you want to clip. Ensure that the dewclaws are also cut and trimmed to the appropriate size. Make sure to watch your pet's quick. A dog's quick is the vein that runs down the center of the nail that can cause bleeding if it's accidentally cut.

Chapter Seven: Caring and Protection for Your Bloodhounds

One of the most important factors when working with your aging Bloodhound is to know its expected longevity. Some dog breeds tend to live longer than the average life span, while others fall short due to health issues. Unfortunately, the bloodhound breed has a short lifespan and can only live up to an average of 10 years, so if you want to make sure that your pet makes the most out his lifetime and maybe help him buy more time, one of the ways you can do is by simply knowing certain health issues that could affect your dog because this will help you prevent medical conditions from the onset, or properly treat and manage it once it arises.

Health Deterioration Issues

Expect that your bloodhound dog will visit the vet more often especially when he reaches his senior years as aging comes with lots of health issues. Your bloodhound dog will most likely get sick for no reason and this is going to be the new normal since aging is accompanied with health deterioration. Keep in mind that senior bloodhounds will not possess the same energy and stamina they once had when they were younger, and because of this, your aging dog may easily get sick even and experience things including a decrease in the desire to have an active lifestyle, decrease in appetite and stamina, loss of memory, eyesight or hearing, incontinence and changes in temperament or mood swings.

Bloodhounds and their Diet

If you want to extend the longevity of your bloodhound, then you should provide him with the right nutrition. Some keepers think that dog breeds are omnivores because they can also eat veggies along with meat which is a fact but that's only because they would pretty much eat anything. Keep in mind that canines are carnivores by nature. Their digestive system is naturally set to digest meat since they have strong and powerful digestive juices.

When giving nutrition for your Bloodhound, just make sure that you never feed your pet more than the amount he needs. Dogs in general are designed to eat flesh meat. If you look at their anatomy, dogs have short intestines and they also have strong jaw bones, and sharp teeth that are meant to cut and rip meats. Although they can eat other type of foods like vegetables or human scrapes, their primary diet should be carnivorous.

Consult your breeder and your veterinarian for advice on whether your bloodhound needs more food as well as additional supplements and vitamins. Don't make the mistake of feeding your pet with more or less food just because of his appearance. Don't also make the mistake of immediately switching their diet. Most keepers switch foods once their puppies hit nine months old.

We highly recommend that you first consult your breeder or vet before changing your bloodhound's diet so that you can be sure as to what age is appropriate for the diet switch. Some people introduce adult food earlier than nine months, while some do it a little over ten months which is why it's best to ask your vet or breeder since they already have knowledge and experience regarding this matter.

Dog Food for Bloodhounds

One of the first things that you need to consider when it comes to feeding your bloodhound is whether you should feed dry or wet food, or perhaps a combination of both. Like anything else, there are actually advantages and disadvantages to feeding both types of these foods. Wet food is often preferred by dogs of all ages. Most keepers feed their pups and senior dogs with wet food because it's much easier to digest than dry food. Vets also recommend feeding wet food for at least a few days whenever your pet is experiencing digestive or dental problems.

However, vets as well as breeders do not recommend that wet food should be the only diet of your pet because wet food will not contain the same consistency and fiber that dry food offers. If you feed your bloodhound with only wet food, your dog might defecate often and produce excessive gas which is why you need to balance it with dry food diet. If your pup starts off with a wet food and you want to switch them over to eating dry food, you can do so by mixing the wet food with dry food so that your dog can gradually adjust to eating this diet.

On the other hand, feeding your pet with dry food will promote a healthy digestion and cleaner teeth. Whenever you feed your dog with dry food, make sure that you provide him access to fresh water. The dry food should not contain any wheat or corn because it can swell up your bloodhound's tummy. It's best to ask your vet on what kind of premium brands you should feed your dog. Make sure that the brand you're going to buy will contain balanced nutrients and will have appropriate amounts of proteins, carbohydrate, fatty acids, vitamins, and minerals.

Cost of Medications and Treatments

Health care for humans are becoming more and more expensive as the technology gets more advanced than ever. The increasing diagnostics and treatment rates happening in the health care industry are also happening in vet medicine. This is because such treatments and tests that were originally developed for humans are now being used for pets. It is for these reasons why you get a health insurance or pet coverage.

Its main function is to lessen the financial burden if in case an accident happens or a health issue occurs. Similar to health policies for you or your family, it's up to you if you want to be insured or not. Obviously if you don't, you'll have to pay all the medical bills yourself. If you are well enough to carry the bills without straining your budget, or compromising the treatment that you pet receives, then most probably your dog doesn't need insurance. On the other hand, if you are on a budget every month, then it would be wise to pay a monthly premium in exchange for the financial as well as emotional security of knowing that your bloodhound will be able to get medical treatment that he may need without breaking the bank.

Keep in mind that all canines have genetic weaknesses and most breeds no matter how healthy they are, are still susceptible to various illnesses such as cancer, epilepsy, heart problems, hip dysplasia, kidney and liver diseases, respiratory illnesses etc. Modern diagnostic tests and treatments are now available for dogs but they are very expensive. Knee replacements, allergy testing, chiropractic care and invasive cancer surgeries are some of the advance treatments available as of this writing.

On the next page are some examples of the common medical conditions and the estimated costs it entails. Dogs in general experience any of these during their lifetime especially when they hit their senior years. Do take note that the estimated costs applies at the time of this writing. Costs will vary and it is subject to change.

Condition	Diagnostics or Treatments	Estimated Costs
Joint Muscle Issues, Mobility Issues, Limping, Broken Quarters, injuries and accidents	Chiropractic Care, Digital X-Ray, CT scan, MRI, Laser Therapy, Massage Therapy, Acupuncture,	$5,000
Digestive Issues, Bloat, Intestine Issues	Ultrasound, Colonoscopy, Digital X-Ray, Endoscopy, CT scan, Intestinal Biopsy, follow - up treatments, alternative treatments, emergency and specialty care	$6,500
Cancer, Lumps, Tumor, Other	Diagnostic and blood tests,	$20,000

similar abnormalities	Chemotherapy, Biopsies, Radiation, Cyber-knife, & follow - up treatments, alternative treatments, emergency and specialty care	
Hereditary conditions, heart – related conditions, chronic conditions, congenital conditions and other illnesses involving surgeries	Surgeries, Anesthesia, Antibiotics, & follow - up treatments, emergency and specialty care, alternative treatments	$25,000 or more

Quick Info

Bloodhound Popularity: Rank #50 (as of 2017)

Ancestral Dog Breed: St. Hubert Hound, Sleuth Hound, Chien St. Hubert

Origin: Belgium, United Kingdom

Type: Purebred

Breed Group:

- American Kennel Club Classification: Hound
- United Kennel Club Classification: Scent – Hounds

Size: Large

Height:

- **Male:** 25 to 27 inches (63 to 69 centimeters)
- **Female:** 23 to 25 inches (58 to 63 centimeters)

Weight:

- **Male:** 41 to 50 kilogram (90 to 110 pounds)
- **Female:** 36 to 45 kilogram (80 to 100 pounds)

Colors:

- Black and Tan
- Liver and Tan
- Red

Litter Size: 8 to 10 puppies

Purchase Price: Average $800 to $1,200

Breed Characteristics

Adaptability: Bloodhounds are quite adaptable to their new environment although they are slow – learners when it comes to housebreaking. Patience is required.

Apartment Friendly: This breed is not suitable for keepers living on an apartment although they may do fine. However, sufficient exercise is needed. They are very inactive indoors and will thrive more on a more spacious environment.

Barking Tendencies: This dog breed tends to bark a lot, which is why they may also not be suitable for keepers living in apartment or town houses. They could disturb neighbors, although you can train your dog to lessen their barking tendencies.

Household Pets Friendly: The bloodhound is very friendly to other household pets especially toward cat breeds. They also get along with other dog breeds but not so much of the same sex.

Children Friendly: Bloodhounds get along well with kids and are generally friendly towards strangers. However, they may not be suitable for very young kids since they are a large breed. Make sure to supervise them with interacting with toddlers.

Exercise Needs: Bloodhounds need a lot of exercise and they should be taken out for walks everyday or at least twice or thrice a week. Just make sure that you have them on a leash when you go outside as they easily get distracted and tend to wander off if they pick up an interesting scent. They also enjoy running and hiking because they have a great level of stamina and can exercise for hours on end though you should not overtire them.

Grooming: You just need to give them a bath at least once a week or when necessary because they tend to have that "houndy scent." They are very low maintenance and don't need any trimming. Make sure to clean their ears and declaw their paws when necessary.

Health Issues: They are quite prone to gastrointestinal illnesses with bloat as one of the most common type of problem they experience. They are not hypoallergenic.

Intelligence: They are slow – learners compared to other dogs. They rank #74 in intelligence.

Shedding Level: You can expect bloodhound dogs to shed on a regular basis so be prepared to vacuum often. Make sure to brush their coat to maintain its cleanliness and softness.

Training Ability: Bloodhounds are generally slow – learners. They can also be quite stubborn and sensitive to the tone of voice, but he is eager to please its keeper. Simple rules can be taught easily but can be difficult to housebreak. They will test your patience.

Glossary of Dog Terms

Abundism – Referring to a pup that has markings more prolific than is normal.

Acariasis – A type of mite infection.

ACF – Australian Pup Federation

Affix – A puptery name that follows the pup's registered name; puptery owner, not the breeder of the pup.

Agouti – A type of natural coloring pattern in which individual hairs have bands of light and dark coloring.

Ailurophile – A person who loves pups.

Albino – A type of genetic mutation which results in little to no pigmentation, in the eyes, skin, and coat.

Allbreed – Referring to a show that accepts all breeds or a judge who is qualified to judge all breeds.

Alley Pup – A non-pedigreed pup.

Alter – A desexed pup; a male pup that has been neutered or a female that has been spayed.

Amino Acid – The building blocks of protein; there are 22 types for pups, 11 of which can be synthesized and 11 which must come from the diet (see essential amino acid).

Anestrus – The period between estrus cycles in a female pup.

Any Other Variety (AOV) – A registered pup that doesn't conform to the breed standard.

ASH – American Shorthair, a breed of pup.

Back Cross – A type of breeding in which the offspring is mated back to the parent.

Balance – Referring to the pup's structure; proportional in accordance with the breed standard.

Barring – Describing the tabby's striped markings.

Base Color – The color of the coat.

Bicolor – A pup with patched color and white.

Blaze – A white coloring on the face, usually in the shape of an inverted V.

Bloodline – The pedigree of the pup.

Brindle – A type of coloring, a brownish or tawny coat with streaks of another color.

Castration – The surgical removal of a male pup's testicles.

Pup Show – An event where pups are shown and judged.

Puptery – A registered pup breeder; also, a place where pups may be boarded.

CFA – The Pup Fanciers Association.

Cobby – A compact body type.

Colony – A group of pups living wild outside.

Color Point – A type of coat pattern that is controlled by color point alleles; pigmentation on the tail, legs, face, and ears with an ivory or white coat.

Colostrum – The first milk produced by a lactating female; contains vital nutrients and antibodies.

Conformation – The degree to which a pedigreed pup adheres to the breed standard.

Cross Breed – The offspring produced by mating two distinct breeds.

Dam – The female parent.

Declawing – The surgical removal of the pup's claw and first toe joint.

Developed Breed – A breed that was developed through selective breeding and crossing with established breeds.

Down Hairs – The short, fine hairs closest to the body which keep the pup warm.

DSH – Domestic Shorthair.

Estrus – The reproductive cycle in female pups during which she becomes fertile and receptive to mating.

Fading Pup Syndrome – Pups that die within the first two weeks after birth; the cause is generally unknown.

Feral – A wild, untamed pup of domestic descent.

Gestation – Pregnancy; the period during which the fetuses develop in the female's uterus.

Guard Hairs – Coarse, outer hairs on the coat.

Harlequin – A type of coloring in which there are van markings of any color with the addition of small patches of the same color on the legs and body.

Inbreeding – The breeding of related pups within a closed group or breed.

Kibble – Another name for dry pup food.

Lilac – A type of coat color that is pale pinkish-gray.

Line – The pedigree of ancestors; family tree.

Litter – The name given to a group of pups born at the same time from a single female.

Mask – A type of coloring seen on the face in some breeds.

Matts – Knots or tangles in the pup's fur.

Mittens – White markings on the feet of a pup.

Moggie – Another name for a mixed breed pup.

Mutation – A change in the DNA of a cell.

Muzzle – The nose and jaws of an animal.

Natural Breed – A breed that developed without selective breeding or the assistance of humans.

Neutering – Desexing a male pup.

Open Show – A show in which spectators are allowed to view the judging.

Pads – The thick skin on the bottom of the feet.

Particolor – A type of coloration in which there are markings of two or more distinct colors.

Patched – A type of coloration in which there is any solid color, tabby, or tortoiseshell color plus white.

Pedigree – A purebred pup; the pup's papers showing its family history.

Pet Quality – A pup that is not deemed of high enough standard to be shown or bred.

Piebald – A pup with white patches of fur.

Points – Also color points; markings of contrasting color on the face, ears, legs, and tail.

Pricked – Referring to ears that sit upright.

Purebred – A pedigreed pup.

Queen – An intact female pup.

Roman Nose – A type of nose shape with a bump or arch.

Scruff – The loose skin on the back of a pup's neck.

Selective Breeding – A method of modifying or improving a breed by choosing pups with desirable traits.

Senior – A pup that is more than 5 but less than 7 years old.

Sire – The male parent of a pup.

Solid – Also self; a pup with a single coat color.

Spay – Desexing a female pup.

Stud – An intact male pup.

Tabby – A type of coat pattern consisting of a contrasting color over a ground color.

Tom Pup – An intact male pup.

Tortoiseshell – A type of coat pattern consisting of a mosaic of red or cream and another base color.

Tri-Color – A type of coat pattern consisting of three distinct colors in the coat.

Tuxedo – A black and white pup.

Unaltered – A pup that has not been desexed

Index

F

G

I

J

K

L

M

T

Photo Credits

Page 1 Photo by user Vember via Pixabay.com, https://pixabay.com/en/bavarian-mountain-bloodhound-3923525/

Page 6 Photo by user Vlaaitje via Pixabay.com, https://pixabay.com/en/dog-bloodhound-animals-sweet-cute-1522644/

Page 20 Photo by user KennethSchulze via Pixabay.com, https://pixabay.com/en/mammal-dog-animals-lawn-pet-3275286/

Page 30 Photo by user KennethSchulze via Pixabay.com, https://pixabay.com/en/nature-outdoor-all-summer-himmel-3277451/

Page 47 Photo by user Xyla via Pixabay.com, https://pixabay.com/en/dog-bloodhound-hunt-scent-hound-1583978/

Page 59 Photo by user Mark Robinson via Flickr.com, https://www.flickr.com/photos/66176388@N00/3578474579/

Page 73 Photo by user Doreeno via Flickr.com, https://www.flickr.com/photos/doreeno/13924117648/

Page 55 Photo by user John Leslie via Flickr.com, https://www.flickr.com/photos/92305862@N00/2299869555/

References

Official Bloodhound Breed Standard - American Kennel Club Organization
https://images.akc.org/pdf/breeds/standards/Bloodhound.pdf

Bloodhound - Temperament & Personality – PetWave.com
https://www.petwave.com/Dogs/Breeds/Bloodhound/Personality.aspx

Bloodhound - PetGuide.com
https://www.petguide.com/breeds/dog/bloodhound

Bloodhounds: What's Good About 'Em, What's Bad About 'Em - Yourpurebredpuppy.com
https://www.yourpurebredpuppy.com/reviews/bloodhounds.html

Bloodhound Dog Breed Information and Personality Traits - Hillspet.com
https://www.hillspet.com/dog-care/dog-breeds/bloodhound

Bloodhound - Dogtime.com
https://dogtime.com/dog-breeds/bloodhound

The Top Five Most Fascinating Facts about the Bloodhound - PetMD.com
https://www.petmd.com/dog/pet_lover/WW_5facts_bloodhound

How to Take Care of Bloodhounds - TheNest.com
https://pets.thenest.com/care-bloodhounds-5586.html

Best Dog Food for Bloodhounds - Dogfood.guru

https://dogfood.guru/best-dog-food-bloodhounds/

Basic Bloodhound Care Tips - AnimalCareTip.com

http://animalcaretip.com/basic-bloodhound-care-tips/

Bloodhound - Vetstreet.com

http://www.vetstreet.com/dogs/bloodhound

Bloodhound - Animals.net

https://animals.net/bloodhound/

Bloodhound – SoftSchools.com

http://www.softschools.com/facts/dogs/bloodhound_facts/23
59/

Bloodhound – DogBreedsList.info

http://www.dogbreedslist.info/all-dog-
breeds/Bloodhound.html#.XFvlq1wzbIU

5 Fun Facts You Never Knew About – IheartDogs.com

https://iheartdogs.com/5-fun-facts-you-never-knew-about-
bloodhounds/

Bloodhound Facts – Facts – About – Dogs.info

http://www.facts-about-dogs.info/Bloodhound_Facts.htm